My ABCs of Af

Northern Africa

Algeria · Egypt · Lybia · Morocco · Sudan · Tunisia · Western Sahara

Eastern Africa

Burundi · Comoros · Djibouti · Eritrea · Ethiopia · Kenya · Madagascar
Malawi · Mauritius · Mayotte(France) · Mozambique · Reunion(France) · Rwanda · Seychelles
Somalia · South Sudan · Tanzania · Uganda · Zambia · Zimbabwe

Central Africa

Angola · Cameroon · Central African Republic · Chad
D. R. of the Congo · Rep. of the Congo · Equatorial Guinea · Gabon · São Tomé and Príncipe

Southern Africa

Botswana · Lesotho · Namibia · South Africa · Swaziland

Western Africa

Benin · Burkina Faso · Cape Verde · Gambia · Ghana · Guinea
Guinea-Bissau · Ivory Coast · Liberia · Mali · Mauritania · Niger · Nigeria · Saint Helena, Ascension and Tristan da Cunha (United Kingdom) · Senegal · Sierra Leone · Togo

Northern Africa

Western Africa

Central Africa

Eastern Africa

Southern Africa

My ABC's of Africa

Dr. Jasoe Sharpe Hargrove

Dedication

This book is dedicated to HGS.
Thank you for being the best daddy and
mentor anyone could have.
Love you, Papay!

Acknowledgment

Thank you to everyone who contributed somehow to the success of this project. To Kathy and Nathan, thank you for being available instantly upon my requests for help. To Martina, I know how annoying and demanding I got during this project, you are one of a kind and I appreciate you.

Africa is the second largest continent and second most populated continent in the world. It is extremely rich with a vast variety of traditions, landforms, animals, plants, cultures, religions and climates. There are 54 countries in Africa with over 1.2 billion people speaking over 1,000 languages.

The Sub-Saharan region of Africa has the most diverse taxonomy of bird species in the world. Approximately 25% of all the world's birds are found in Africa. The largest, tallest and heaviest bird in the world, the ostrich, is indigenous to Africa.

A calabash is a gourd plant that serves many purposes in most African homes. This plant grows in every African country. Once harvested, it is opened, hallowed-out and dried before usage. Some well-known usage of the calabash includes home decors, musical instruments and handling food.

Dd
is for Djembe

Music plays a significant role in Africa and has been used for many purposes including communication and ritualistic purposes. Djembe is a prominent musical instrument that originated in Mali and Guinea. This percussion instrument is usually played using the bare hands and has three major sounds- bass, slap and tone.

Ee is for Eland

The Eland, one of the world's largest antelopes, is found in the eastern and southern grassland of Africa. They can weigh up to 2,200 pounds, live up to 20 years and their spiral horns can grow up to 3 feet tall.

The Fish River Canyon is the second largest canyon in the world. It is south of Africa in Namibia. This canyon is approximately 100 miles long, 16 miles wide and 340 miles deep. The Fish River Canyon is usually dried most times of the year except during the rainy season months of January to April.

Gg
is for Goliath Frog

The goliath frog, the world's largest frog, is also a habitant of Africa. The body of the goliath frog can grow up to approximately 12 inches long and weigh about 7 pounds. This frog can be found mostly in Cameroon and Equatorial Guinea along fast moving water.

Hh

is for Hippopotamus

Another record sized animal indigenous to Africa is the Hippopotamus. The hippopotamus is the third largest land mammal in the world. This semi-aquatic animal measures up to about 15 feet long, 5 feet tall and 4 tons heavy. Hippopotamus can be found only in the sub-Saharan region of Africa.

Imbe, also known as wild plum or African mangosteen, is a very
unpopular fruit grown in the warm parts of Africa from Somalia to
Guinea. This fruit is a sweet fruit that can be made into jam,
jelly and other preserves. Imbe is little known mainly because of
the difficulty in transporting due to how badly it stains.

Jj

is for Jollof Rice

African staple is as diverse as everything else in Africa. Rice is a staple that is prominent in most countries. Jollof Rice is a common cuisine in most West African countries. This meal is a one-pot meal that contains a variety of meat, vegetables and different types of spices.

Kk
is for Kola nut

Kola Nut is a naturally caffeinated fruit grown in the tropical rainforests of Africa. It is used in flavoring beverages with cola. This fruit is significant in most African countries because of its medicinal value.

Liberia is Africa's first republic. She declared her independence in 1847. In 2006, Liberia became the first nation in Africa to elect a female president – Ellen Johnson Sirleaf.

Mansa Kankan Musa is known to be one of Africa's greatest rulers. He ruled the empire of Mali from 1307 to 1337. It is said that Mansa Musa is the richest man to ever live. His net worth exceeded 400 billion USD. He was also well known for his generosity. He shared his wealth with rulers of other empires.

Nn
is for Nile River

The Nile River, which is over 4,000 miles long, is the longest river in the world. This river originates south of the equator and flows northward draining into the Mediterranean Sea. The Nile River is home to the world's largest freshwater reptile and second largest crocodile in the world – The Nile Crocodile.

Oo

is for Okapi

Okapi is a rare animal found in the dense forest of central Africa, mainly in Congo.   With a body like a horse and strips like a zebra, this solitaire animal is one of the only relatives of the giraffe family.   They can grow up to approximately 5 feet tall and weigh between 400 and 700 pounds.

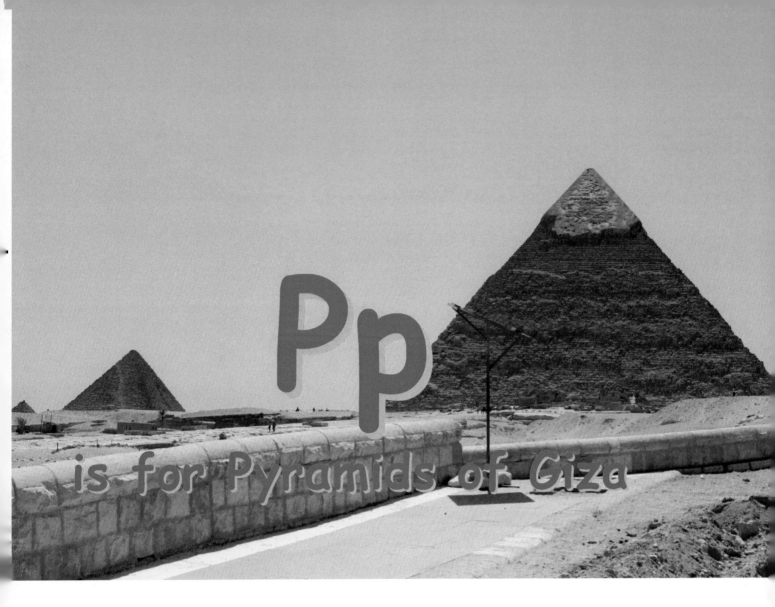

The Pyramids of Giza, one of the seven wonders of the ancient world, is found in Egypt. Pyramids were royal tombs built for Pharaohs and their families for life after death. Although Egypt is well know for Pyramids, Sudan has the most amount of Pyramids in Africa.

Qq

is for Queen Nzinga

ANY ZINGHA,
Queen of Matamba

Queen Anna Nzinga was the Queen of Ndongo and Matamba kingdoms of Angola from 1624 to 1663. She was referred to as the African Warrior Queen because of her fight against the compelling of her people into slavery. She spent most of her time resisting the Portuguese and putting an end to their capturing of Africans and forcing them into slavery.

The Rainforest of Africa covers over 2.2 million square miles stretching across 31 countries within East, West and Central Africa. The African rainforest is home to over 8 thousand species of plants. The oil palm and the mahogany trees are two well-known trees found in the African Rainforest.

Ss

is for Sahara Desert

The Sahara Desert, located in northern Africa, is the world's largest hot desert. It is bordered by the Red Sea to the east, the Mediterranean Sea to the north and the Atlantic Ocean to the west. The area of the Sahara desert is 3.6 million miles, covering 11 countries.

is for Timbuktu

Timbuktu is a city in Mali. This city is home to the world's first university, the University of Sankoré. During the 14th Century, Timbuktu was a very important place for education and commerce. People from different works of life came here to learn and trade.

Uu
is for Uganda

Uganda, an east African landlocked country, is referred to as the "Pearl of Africa." It has earned this name because of its beautiful sceneries, abundance wildlife and several world wonders. This African nation is home to over half of the world's mountain gorillas.

Vv

is for Victoria Falls

The Victoria Falls is one of the seven natural wonders of the world. It is one mile wide and 355 feet high. This beautiful prominent waterfall sits between Zambia and Zimbabwe.

Ww is for Witwatersrand Basin

In addition to beautiful landscapes, vast cultures, and abundant animals, Africa is also extremely rich in natural and mineral resources. The world's largest gold resource is in Africa. Witwatersrand Basin, a city in South Africa, prides itself as the only location where over half the world's gold has been mined.

Xx
is for Xhosa

The Xhosa ethnic group is the second largest culture group in South Africa. The Xhosa language is spoken in the Eastern Cape of South Africa and is also taught in schools. Nelson Mandela was a descendent of the Xhosa ethnic group.

Yy
is for Yoruba

The Yoruba people are one of the largest ethnic groups in Africa. They extend through various countries in West Africa mostly in Nigeria, Eastern Benin and Togo. The Yoruba people are known for their carving which has become some of the most popular and influential African arts.

Zz

is for Zanzibar

Zanzibar is an archipelago of Tanzania known for its beautiful white sandy beaches. The Arabs heavily influence the culture and traditions of this island. Zanzibar was used as a midway for the African, Arab and European spice and slave trades.

My ABCs of Africa

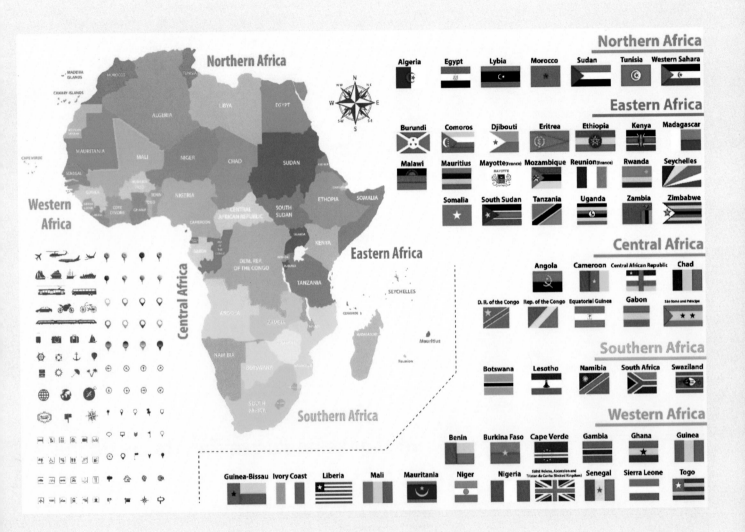

Alena & Jamison

Thanks for choosing
to read about Africa.

signature

Made in the USA
San Bernardino, CA
16 August 2018